THE COLLECTOR OF SHADOWS

THE COLLECTOR
OF SHADOWS

POEMS

James Silas Rogers

2019

Brighthorse Books
13202 N. River Drive
Omaha, NE 68112

ISBN: 978-1-944467-16-6

Cover image: © Jamie Heiden 2018
Author photo: Margaret M. Rogers

For permission to reproduce selections from
this book and for more information about
Brighthorse Books and the Brighthorse Prize,
visit us on the web at brighthorsebooks.com.

For Joe and Mary—the very best

CONTENTS

THE COLLECTOR OF SHADOWS

Chattering starlings in lycra,
the cyclists gather over coffee
on the first day of January.

They talk of last year's totals,
of goals for the twelve months ahead;
gossip about a friend sitting today out,

laugh at another who last night went
for a ride at one minute after midnight,
to be first in their game of distance

unhitched from purpose. Their pleasure
consists of pushing on and coping.
Winter brings grit on the roads,

wipeouts on the ice, faces assaulted
by a needle-prick wind, trails
that go missing under the building snow.

Earnest as infantrymen discussing
frostbite, they laugh together. No one
asks if, or why, the rounds will resume.

The cyclists show no doubts. Hobbling
out the door in cleated shoes, they assume
the welcomed burden of another year.

The new year arrives,
neither a blank check
nor a forgiven debt,

but only as afternoon
sun and shadow
on the backyard snow,

and, just like last year,
clouds in the west move
toward this arbitrary life

where, despite the single-digit
cold, icicles drip off
the south-facing eaves,

and where small, inverted
cups of snow fill in
between the fence pickets.

AWAKENED BY SNOWPLOWS

At night the snowplows crash around
like movie dinosaurs, scraping, shoving,

making an unholy show of their will
to finish the job at hand. They intrude

on sleep like dreams of assured misfortune:
those dreams involving the pull of a waterfall,

or high open rooftops in a gale-force wind,
or the ones in which you've been falsely charged

with a crime, convicted in a show trial.
Out there in the white world, two-ton blades

thunder and press ahead, restoring
the city's grid in scrawled straight lines.

And then the noise fades. You return to sleep,
return to the empty abundance of the dark.

As I cross the river the radio says it's fourteen below.
The defroster fan whines. Snow groans beneath car wheels.
The morning puts me in mind of my fifth-grade reader
and a Paul Bunyan tale of a lumbercamp so cold
that when the loggers spoke the woods stayed silent except
for the tinkle of frozen words breaking like dropped wineglasses
on the forest floor. I glance toward the bridge
that marks the other bracket of my summer cycling loop:
great still plumes hang above smokestacks, fixed upon
the windless winter sky. They erode like dry ice
into the daylight. I think of the word *sundogs*,
which is what my father called the parentheses of faint prism
half-enclosing the hazed sun, and how he first heard the term
from a Montana rancher maybe seventy years ago.
Certain words pass hand to hand; knowing its descent,
I hold the word *sundogs* in my mind, admiring it as I might
admire the heft of a pocketwatch held in my palm—
own it, as I can never own the knowledge, part-recalled
from an anthropology text, that a folk belief somewhere
demands a sudden gift whenever you spot a sundog.
No. That's not my tribe. That's not my story.
I wish, though, that I could make you a gift of these sundogs,
or at least of the word that embraces them, names them,
gives them a place in our lives. I wish that I could do more
than throw words into the frozen air.

Though most of the time it's work,
if you have a talent for what they call
"hunkering down," then late January

can afford a sort of contentment—
the sort Thoreau said he found
in the Maine woods, or which travelers

report on ocean crossings.
These weeks, we scavenge through long
winter days to find a flourish

that redeems this hard season: how
the sun, like a backlit scrim,
might glow through the afternoon gray.

Once in a while, a surprise:
a red-shouldered hawk in the back yard
tearing apart a squirrel's carcass;

later, a band of cirrus clouds
ribbed with the same pale marbling
of that hawk's breast feathers.

And later still, you recall the look
of icy wildness as it lifted its wings—
a whisper of another world.

CROWS IN EARLY WINTER
(NEAR BLACK RIVER FALLS)

Pulling away from the roadside rest,
and the bronzed account of passenger pigeons
netted by the clumsy million
in just these woods,
I enter the flow of traffic
streaming south, carried along
like a twig tossed onto a current.

Crows pass overhead, indifferent to me,
to the road, to the story of the pigeons.
They are weaving their own net,
it seems, headed this way or that
with an intent of their own.

I think I know what the crows know:
the land will belong to them:
the halted fields,
the absurd billboards urging us
to some estival foolishness, the brown
stubble; the snow growing
icy in the winter sun.

A slow storytelling of crows in the air
reclaims this leftover land.

SLOW COOKER

Already this morning we know
that after five, when it will be dark
and maybe even snowing,

we will come indoors, take off
our coats, and be glad of a ready meal.
One of us will set out the green bowls

we always use, and later, the other
will do the dishes without being asked.
Life is often like that: moments

that have never happened before
denoted by small ceremonies
that have always happened—planting a tree,

lighting a candle, closing a coffin lid,
holding a newborn child close.
And also the business of making soup,

a bridge between that which is at hand
and that which we assume.
Though I still need to think about

whether to include tomatoes,
I throw in onions, carrots, sliced
garlic, the left-over hambone

and a can of kidney beans; use too much
pepper, too little salt, and go long
on the thyme (lately I cannot get enough

of thyme). Somehow, over the day,
it will all come together. We know it will.
Our trust goes into that word "slow."

LATE NIGHT, IN KILKENNY

I was trying to remember the name of the arctic bird
that flies the farthest, nearly from pole
to pole, as if hungry for daylight. It was almost
two in the morning. You were an ocean
and a half-continent away. Two in the morning,
and me fumbling to recall the name of that plover
or shorebird; but I was certain, then, that I knew the order
and the rhythms of your day, our places ruptured
but still linked. I knew what you were doing
back in Minnesota, the dinner you likely made,
when you'd go to bed. Crossing the River Nore
in the foggy Irish dark, I saw seabirds in a cluster,
twenty or thirty gulls and terns arranged on a shelf of ice
downstream, arranged as tidy as a place setting
or knick-knacks on some old woman's mantle.
Here in Kilkenny, the Guinness and the lateness
of the hour stirred my thoughts, going over the bridge,
got them muddied up with those birds, who travel
such extraordinary distance, who are so motionless
on the ice. All this made a kind of sense at the time.
This morning all I am is lonely.

MARRIAGE

I learned this on my honeymoon,
driving north toward Grand Marais:
a process of several billion years
explained by a roadside plaque
no bigger than a dishtowel.
The lake is here, it seems, because
at some point back when God was young
His earth compulsively puked lava,
emptied itself out, unable to stop.
For eons it extruded molten rock
by the ton and then the megaton
until at last so much had poured out
that there was nothing underneath
to sustain the inconceivable weight.
Underpinned by air, it collapsed
in a basin: the greatest, most daunting,
and deepest of lakes.

From the kitchen:
a knife butts into a cutting board.
Scallions or carrots sliced
into small segments line up;

a circle of gas bound
by enameled steel
announces itself in a rush,
then the pop of caught flame;

and the vaguely sexual slurp
of a whirling spoon in a bowl,
blending together oil,
lemon juice, a spice;

and the click, click,
of the table being set,
plates with unspoken rightness
into familiar places.

Like the sleepwalker
who attends to the unseen,
I follow these ordinary sounds—
eyes open or not.

OUTSIDE TROTTER'S CAFE

Coffee, and the music of what happens
washing in uneven tides
over sidewalk and street:
not quite audible, not yet found
by the traffic as it moves and halts.

Each day at twenty to eight
a pretty girl in 400 dollars'
worth of clothes gets into her Ford
and grinds the starter.
It rasps, then catches at last.

She segues off, into her world,
as other drivers pass, already
at work with cell phones
to their ears. What can there be
to say at this early hour?

East-facing windows reflect
the climbing sun. An unready man
walks in, necktie not yet knotted.
A woman uses the gift
of a red light to fuss with her hair.

Coffee, and again we take it on trust
that this day, like every day, will in time
find its way, will compose itself anew
out of the morning's assumptions,
the morning's small doubts.

Pond water remembers.
It welcomes back Canadas,
coots, the redwings and their trill;
it waits for the peepers in hope.
It remembers the day each year
when nothing remains to melt,
remembers the half-life of ice
splintering into honeycombs.
Pond water remembers
the shape of the shore,
remembers to rise into the reeds.
It knows that last year's green
will be captured by mud
and finds comfort in the triumph of rot.
Pond water remembers the rain
and is grateful when it falls,
grateful like a runner
drinking deep at the end of a race.
Pond water surrenders to ripples,
opens its palms to feel
the winds and the breeze,
the kisses of dragonflies.

NOT FISHING

When my brother would take the car
to flycast on the Rush River
or the Willow, I'd often ride along.

In hand-me-down hipboots,
I walked the streams alone, battling
the pressure of the current on my thighs

while he spent hours at the big hole
casting. I would wade elsewhere,
not carrying a flyrod. I'd sit on rocks,

straining to hear a music
in the water's all-day spill and gurgle,
well aware that the river flowed

whether or not I attended its sounds.
Dragonflies darted near, darted off,
straws of turquoise and green.

I knew other men fished in this water
and that their words—the hatch,
monofilament, thalweg, and creel—

was speech from which I was detached.
Somehow denied the fishing fraternity,
denied an excuse for my entirely real

love of the river and its ways, I'd sit
to watch the surface-skimming swallows.
the sorties of streamside waxwings.

Still, I knew to admire the ageless stones.

MY GRANDMOTHER'S CHILDHOOD

In each paintless Kentucky
village of her youth,

she cried when wanton
boys turned birds' nests

into litter. Bluebird chicks
spilled as from a kicked bucket

and left to squall, their helpless
chirps lasting the afternoon.

Eggs splattered
like tobacco-spit on a rock.

She wept and was told
there was nothing to weep for.

The boys were only birding.

WAKING UP IN THE HOUSE OF MEN

for the Millers

A warm but not a spring morning,
the sort of March day that drags winter
just behind it like a dirty blanket,

and when I awake, killdeer
peals—the first of the year—
shower out of the sky.

I watch the Zumbro River
as my hosts, a father and son
finding their way back to dailiness,

make breakfast. Her absence
still sits at table with them,
but they will not cry today.

Here is a house of men who say
grace; men who embrace, bravely
and with resignation, their new

ceremonies of ground coffee; men
whose trust in God is as lumpy
and as certain as morning oatmeal.

A bicyclist pushes into the wind
on Holy Saturday morning;
he wants, he needs, dry clothes,
a hot bath to erase this cold ride.
He shivers, cranks harder,
bites his way home through the rain.

This is an unexpected morning,
unexpected for all of us;
a week that ran backwards,
outrageous earliness of spring
reversed for now. Handbrakes
fail in the rain. We're unprepared

but it does not feel wrong,
not today. We haven't fallen
for the pathetic fallacy. No law says
that Easter has to come with sunlight
and lilies or demands that the sky
and grass make an April dazzle.

A cold front from Canada
has moved in, I don't know
for how long. I remember that
this is the last day of Lent
and realize not much has changed.
That cyclist fighting the rain:

at least he is out on the road
even if he didn't know how to dress.
Driving past him I wince
to imagine his rain-soaked shirt,
the icewater down his back,
both of us headed east on Summit.

ANEMOCHORY

This was after the footpath
at the Ford Bridge's end,
where you come out
on the gap of the river valley:

one of those mornings when
sunlight clean as wine
seems poured like a varnish
over the suddenly

green world. A rush of leaves
flashed in the treetops
below. On the river,
a buoy split the current

in a fishtail. It was the air
that I most felt; warm now,
alive with cottonwood seeds
making idle trails

lifting and falling, like grains
in a crystal colloid,
drifting in fathoms of space,
tugged and nudged by forces

too subtle to discern;
riding the breath of morning,
scarcely distinct from that
in which they floated.

AT THE FALLS OF ST. ANTHONY

April nineteenth, nearing dark.
A mist that smells of mud, the sort
you'd clear with one sweep of the wipers
if it came to rest on your windshield,
drifts onto the line of watchers stopped
here and there along the bridge rail.
On the east bank, above the city's oldest
streets (now only restaurants and sushi bars),
a neon sign flashes *St. Anthony Main*.
To the west, in million-dollar condos,
a few enjoy the view from their balcony.
The evening sun falls on it all, and on me,
a middle-aged man walking among
the young and old. Cyclists spin by
and runners following their own circuits
pass in a nimbus of aerobic health.
A couple engages in the ageless ceremony
of flirtation, she with a sky-blue sweater
draped over her shoulders like a vestment,
like the costume of another country.
A handful of young parents are out, too,
with their children strapped in strollers
and slumped to one side, asleep.
As the moms and dads take a moment
to stand and wonder at falling water,
they keep one hand on the stroller
handle, rocking it back and forth
as the river passes underneath. We all gaze
on the torrent. A hundred currents
collect; some quick, others dragging
like slag on a vat of steel. I look on the couple
next to me—he stands at her back, arms
around her waist—and imagine that
we each find ourselves lost in the task

of trying to track one or another
of the streams that meld here at the brim
of the spillway. The northern half of the state
pours to this point, the spring run-off
having scoured not just the snowpack,
but also bridges, trees, islands, some farmers'
best acres, now missing, lost into the Mississippi,
"indistinct as water is in water." Antony's words.
Not the saint whose name was given
to these falls, but the love-mad Roman.
Utterly different men and, yet, both tried
to understand where things go
when they vanish. The question occurs
to me as well, watching the cold water drop.
The dark river swallows the river,
and no amount of praying, not even
to the patron saint of lost objects,
can bring it back.

Oh, my America.
This is where the lost continent went.

THE APRIL MAN

Each year he emerges about the time snipe
return to the cobalt lakes and the canebrakes.

There is something crazy about the April man.
The world frustrates him more than most,

makes him twitch with impatience,
impels him to re-assert his worst mistakes.

The April man eats pie filling from a can
for breakfast, having bought it by the crate.

He cuts his own hair in the dark, and yet is vain.
He complains without stop about small things—

a switchplate placed too low on the wall
or a gas station that no longer stays open late—

but he sleeps on the floor in a room without heat.
Yes, something went wrong for the April man.

Blame the winter. Blame the long months alone.
Blame the bare trees. Blame the hint

of malice in the April winds. Blame the snow
that falls on him as on an empty street.

WINDOW KILLS

for Joan Cox

After we had gone through the closet, winnowing
all but the finest of clothes (suitable to be buried in,
was our unspoken thought), and allowed the bills
to arrive in a bolus at month's end until unforeseen
debts could no longer slap us in the face; after
we had pieced together an address book of sorts
out of old envelopes and paper scraps tucked in the desk;
after we'd come to believe we had tidied up
our mother's life, we opened the freezer.

In the frosty dark we found a dozen or more bird
cadavers, songbirds that had dropped x number of stories
to the street, only feathers to cushion their crash landing.
When Icarus fell there was at least a sense that balance
had been restored, hubris given its due comeuppance.
Not so these fallen creatures. The worst this purple finch
had done was mistake its reflection for another bird,
and lost that game of flinch. Hardly a capital offense,
to be misled, but office towers scarcely care.

But she did. Taxidermy may be a feeble hope
yet it was the hope she held. We thought of her lifting
a lifeless bird off the sidewalk, carrying it home in her purse
with her lipstick, her compact, her keys. The poet
was right: Hope *is* the thing with feathers.
She kept her wished-for restoration frozen,
stacked like ears of sweetcorn. Kept a rock-hard
fire-orange oriole. Kept woodpeckers that once could drill
their way through hundred-year oak, found dead
after one sick thud. Kept a bead-emerald hummingbird
that now looked like a sausage encrusted with freezer burn.
And a Redstart that must have been skipping through air
one crystal morning when it simply, suddenly, stopped.

It is their nature, not their will,
how these meager birds compete
for still more meager nourishment.

The sparrows have wings,
but theirs is a peasant's life:
scratching and pecking at spilled

millet husks on the asphalt.
Their hunger is a prison.
The flock scatters when

anything draws close—a boy
on a bicycle, a woman stepping
out of her car—but the birds return

as surely as surf will trickle
back to the edge of the sea,
meeting the next arriving wave.

My father would tend his grill for hours,
its briquettes never flaming. He'd stand

outside from just before sunset until
well after dark, poking, banking up, watching.

Sometimes, for no reason, the coals would glow
hotter, as if exhaling. But mostly

this was an exercise in steadiness,
a solo vigil of his own choosing, and apart.

It is forty years later, and on Sundays now
I do much the same, though with less patience,

using maple twigs, their grey surfaces dry
as shed snakeskins. Every time I bend,

I think of the Drumshanbo house, of a small boy
helping his mother. Of how the dark fell early.

And of how in those moments he was hers.
The boy knew happiness; his pleasure was to gather

small sticks, given to be gone in flames.
The chill of the April evening returns to me.

The guidebook gets some of it right,
though omits how the bird shrugs its wings,
enlarging to flash his gold-edged, scarlet epaulets.
The book neglects the reddening willow switches
or the residuum of last year's swamp, reeds
bending over and fat cattail heads
now crumbling into grains, like pollen.

But the book comes close on the call:
"A gurgling *oak-a-lee*, followed by *chek*."

All the same, paper only takes you so far.
So much more is being said when,
on a concrete path beside the Rock River
a redwing ejaculates its spring-loaded song:
that the earth is always a woman,
and that somehow, somewhere,
and in important ways, we get this wrong.

SCENIC OVERLOOK

for Seán L.

Over mullein stalks and red cedar
that clutched the limestone slope,

a cast of buzzards came dealing
themselves into our day. They poured

across the bluff tops, wheeling
like a skater's silent blades on ice.

Sometimes the ground falls away
and a single thing—a toothache,

a flat tire, a sudden love—
displaces the rest of the world.

Eight scrawny silhouettes
left us wordless, filled the sky.

THE RIVER ROAD, AGAIN

Dandelion crowns
have gone to seed.
The road sketches a ragged line
along the bluff tops.

The river has crested. It runs
as it ran ten thousand years past—
a ladder warblers climb
up the spine of North America.

It is a season for thinking of cycles:
the stop-and-go circling
of the heart turns again.

Leaves not two weeks old
are made new a second time
in the evening sun.

PAST GUESSING

Thirty years on, she still
pulls out an occasional rabbit,

lets it slip that she can hear
a music others never do

or will reach into a place
not just hidden but unlearnable.

I am thinking of a day
when I came home at five P.M.

and my wife told me
she had lain on the floor

since noon beside our dog,
who could barely lift his head

and who shook for some reason
past our guessing.

Sunlight filled the kitchen. She'd run
her hands along his ribs, saying

*you've been a good dog
and can give yourself back to God,*

until, like ripples losing themselves
in a pond, the tremors stopped

and he slept at ease
there on the white linoleum.

It seems right to me now
that her first word was "light."

SUMMER EVENING

My daughter in the pool:
I watch her splash.

A branch of unripe
apples droops full; past

it, a summer sky,
blue as the Virgin's dress.

The chimney swifts
fly low, riding a hatch.

I will remember
this night, will recall

unblemished apples
that have not fallen,

that might not fall.

Bede or some such saint said that all
this earthly life amounts to is a bird
flying in and out the windows of a hall.
That's an arresting thought, this morning
on the ground in this non-place where
the highest good is to be on time
and no one asks what time itself is good for.
Today, Bede might have preferred
to use the metaphor of changing planes;
we hurry around while being transferred
from one gate to another, then sit—
a pinball waiting to be flippered out
of a frozen stasis and onto the scheduled
crest of a tide. On the other hand, the system
works, most of the time, though this morning
is one of those frozen-in spaces, owing
to a mechanical delay. A ten-year-old boy
across from me is immersed in a handheld
game. I wonder if he knows the difference
between his toy reality and the flight
for which we both wait. Do I?
Idling at the gate, the book I am reading
involves medieval wonder tales
of talking birds. They were easy to believe,
nine hundred years ago. An eagle
would climb onto a sinning king's
dinner table and give him a fierce
but pious scolding. Or a white dove
would give comfort at an empty cradle.
Talking crows were common in the olden
days. Such miracles caught no one off guard;
just ordinary stories that got told in
grocery stores and pubs. I closed my book
and as I did, a small feathered blur,

a house sparrow, flew overhead, streaking
straight down the mezzanine. Were
I more optimistic, I'd like to think
the bird could find a way out of its airport stir,
but I concede I have my doubts.
Morning sunlight was pouring through vast
windows, but the bird, like the rest of us
was caught on the inside of the glass—
no weather, no breeze, and I am afraid
no way out. Yet, I thought, just perhaps
this vagrant bird really is a sign. I imagined
a serf in the age of Alfred, and how he might
now and then look up from the mud
to see a passing lark, and be reminded
by its song and its disappearance into
the distance that, yes, escape
was still possible somewhere in the world.
I admit that on Concourse C, I was far
from certain there was any place the sparrow
could go. Still, give credit for effort:
it left a whisper in its wake.

For instance, the physics of red wine,
which Galileo called "sunlight held together
by water." Sounds plausible, but how?
Or backing up a step, with the physics
of beauty itself, such as radiates
in these freshly washed Delaware grapes.
With the possible exception of a woman's
breast, a tumbling cluster of grapes
or the globe of one full fruit
might be as nearly perfect a form
as we will see in this life.
Look at this shoulder of table grapes
in the evening sun. Know that
the old prig St. Augustine,
a too-stern and oh-so-rational man,
was right on this: it was love
that called the world into being.

ON THE CANNON RIVER

for Pat Coleman

Herons, attended only
by their shadows,
stand on low mud slopes,

wait among scuffed
clamshells and gravel at points
where the river bends,

birds alone.
Our quiet, passing canoe
untethers their blue-gray forms.

They lift
and in solemn, slow strokes
row the air, move downstream.

Without wanting,
we chase a great blue for miles,
in pursuit of solitude.

That summer, we saw the barred owl a dozen times,
always in the evening, near the grotto.

It would have selected a branch on which to pause
and be backlit, above us, at maybe twice

the height of a man, moving only now and then
with a pivot of its head. Mosquitoes came in swarms.

We didn't swat or even move, for fear of chasing
the owl away. Watching the owl on those long late days

after the solstice when daylight seems to evaporate
was like watching a bloom about to break—

tense, like a strung instrument now at rest,
taut as the morning stillness of a lake.

Wildflowers, regardless of name, will bloom
without apology, under the names of

helianthus, prairie dock, or something else.
This midafternoon in July, the roadside

is besotted with sprays of ox-eye daisy,
thousands weaving and flickering in the wind,

like midday fireflies. They offer a dare—
to believe the world will not end with us.

And, as it happens, I know a fossil poem
dwells in what we still call the flower: *day's eye*,

the sun, or the someone who watches us all.
Standing here alongside State Highway 13,

knowing the name and its origin confers
some pleasure, though not that much. What I ask

is to remember, when words get overproud,
that loving flowers is the first act of prayer.

When I went for a crowbar downstairs
a bee big as a wine cork
was batting the floorboards and joists,

having come through cracks
in the limestone foundation
to nest in our musty basement.

I emptied a jar of nails, cupped
it over her buzzing form: a snow-globe
whirring with frustration.

Outside, I turned the jar over.
Captivity cast aside, the bee
rose like a spark flying upward.

She lifted toward the sky
like a balloon released
from a child's grasp, then halted

on an apple blossom.
I stood and watched,
forgetting why I needed that crowbar.

CLOTHESLINES

She loves them, not because they symbolize
anything about home, or who she is,
but as things in the world: the spring-loaded pins,
the soggy towels, tee-shirts wrung into ropes,
nuggets of underwear bundled like a child's fist,
the four parallel cords empty in the afternoon sun,
the sag of the line under a wet wall of sheets.
Clotheslines, nothing more.
What she does best is hang out laundry.
When I worry about our too-demanding drafty
old house, worry about dubious neighbors,
and now and then suggest we move,
she replies, *But what about a clothesline?*
The day she came home after surgery,
before she walked through the door, with her wounds
still bandaged, she was at the line, snapping
towels to expel wrinkles, folding pillowcases.
She has a system. She has an axiom she applies to life
as if it were a quilt going over a rumpled bed:
"*Do what you have to do, for beauty's sake.*"
Or that's what I would say it is. Along those lines.
But I know she would put it otherwise:
What she'd say instead is, *Let me hang the laundry.*

Silence after too many words:
that works, too.

A Saturday morning in July, driving
north on Interstate 35, my wife and I,
to bring our daughter home from camp.

Somewhere past the sad subdivisions
near Forest Lake, we passed a swamp,
which I told her I had one time heard
was the southernmost tamarack bog
in Minnesota.

In fact, I don't think she understood
then, or could tell you now,
what a tamarack is.
It did not have to matter.

A brown thrasher flew across
the road, west to east, before
disappearing into the deeper woods.

Two middle-aged parents on the road,
who know everything.

LAYERS

Queen Anne's lace everywhere, the day
we left you and drove back from Illinois.
Along the road to Lincoln, it hung
over all the uncultivated spaces.
between the soybean fields and the shoulders,
like a stratus of morning fog. You deserve
to be remembered by a lovelier flower
than a species of wild carrot spread at random,
nubbly crowns the color of window putty.

Long ago, when you were in your infancy
I told my friend, *I think this is the child
who will break my heart.* How wrong
I was, how wrong. That day in August
I wanted to cry, but cannot be sad
you left for an uncertain Providence;
not even when Queen Anne's lace seizes the land
like an early snow, when its wan flowers scatter
everywhere, like the residue of a flood.

A cyclone fence along the first-
and third-base lines
of an empty baseball field,

covered with bindweed in bloom;
unwanted dark-heart leaves
and white trumpet flowers

spread through the grass, grasp
as weeds do, at the wire.
Too much sun and too much sky:

goldfinches rise
from the outfield grass
like bottle rockets, whistling to each other.

Tough-stemmed plants
claim the wounded lots as their own,
grip fast where there is no topsoil,

filling in after a bulldozer: lambsquarter,
pennycress, wild alyssum, marestail,
curled dock with its nubbly seeds

where nothing ought to grow.
I walked into such a patch
near a strip mall in Davenport, Iowa.

Five thousand starlings
scavenging in the grit.
With every step, a dozen, more,

boiled up from the skinned ground,
the most persistent of birds
blooming from underfoot,

wings flapping, loudly and too near
as if a groundburst explosive
had sprung them into flight.

Yesterday, cycling down
the east shore of Green Lake
I watched as a monarch
descended through the whims
of summer air
in that stretch where
Indian Beach Road makes
a furrow in the trees—
where ashes, oaks, and poplars
grown over with wild cucumber
and who knows
what other vegetation
leave only a narrow carpet of sky.

The monarch was falling the way
a mantra slips from the mind,
with the grace of resignation;
tracing the slow arc you see
when, say, a plate
is dropped in the lake—
the way it flashes, rocks, and maybe
turns over for no reason
before it passes, irresistibly,
into the blackness of deep water.
Its wings stroked ineptly
as it rode down in semicurves,
a halting pendulum.

PREDICTABILITY

There are places in time, moments you know
you will meet again, more or less the same
way you expect to see great blue herons
at the river's edge, or snow at Christmas,
or pillbugs under an overturned rock.

Moments like after the rain: beaded grass,
the clean smell of the still wet asphalt street,
the startle of a scooping nighthawk's bleat.
Or the blackbirds grouping in late August
when the year surrenders to weediness

and you find browning apple husks, emptied
by wasps, on the tree. In unmowed places
blooms of milkweed and boneset hang like clouds.
In the verge of the railroad right-of-way,
the noonday sfumato of goldenrod.

If she could, she would save the best shadows
for future use, roll them up like a throw rug.
She places candles to cast wobbling outlines
around the room, wavering at a breath.

She hangs sun-catchers in the window,
then looks behind to consider where
their shadows fall, delighting that she's made
a dim puppet show dance on the wall.

She treasures the silhouetted leaves of runner
beans cast long across the porch slats at sunset,
the ripples in old glass pouring onto the floor,
the sprinkled light under a locust tree.

And nothing is lost. And nothing is lost.

The sun-starved trunks
of aspens appear upright
as a railway clock fixed at noon,

yet if you stop to watch
you will in time see the trunks
sway, shift in their verticality

when the wind off Lake Superior
reaches this glacial ridge
and brushes the forest crown.

Big Manitou tumbles on, behind.
In the cool of the September
woods, the world looks to halt.

But the world moves. I stand
on my feet, on the earth. Longing
consumes me like a toothache.

One day, in your forties or fifties,
you will start to think that life is turning
into a long string of small extinctions.
You will feel the word *gone* rise inside you
and might even say it aloud, quietly, the way
you would say it if the house had been robbed
and, months later, you reached for an item
you never knew was missing, thought had been
in a drawer the whole time: *Gone.* Add these
to the workaday wrong turns you half-knew
were coming from the start—you know: the shy
girl with trusting eyes with whom
you did not sleep, the dad who let you down—
and you will begin to think that if you started
crying now, you might never be able to stop.
But that doesn't happen.
What happens instead is you make a cup of tea.
You sit on the front porch, and there you look
at spindly asters on a September afternoon:
flowers with ragged edges that are barely petals,
a color from somewhere down the spectrum
after blue—the same blue of cold skies
in early winter. And behind them,
the deep green of bloomless morning glories.

DANDELIONS

i.m. Larry McBride

Only the day before I had hugged
his wife and shared earnest handshakes
with his two fine children. Now,
returning from the wake on county roads
flanked by dandelion-crowded ditches,
for seventy miles or so I was talking
aloud to myself, trying to describe
those weeds in the morning sun.
Mostly the metaphors sounded weak;
salt grains cast across a plate, or seeds
spread wide by a sower's hand. Then it struck
me how, when a storm draws over a lake,
ragged drifts of rain will dapple the surface;
and it pleased me to think
of these useless yellow flowers like that:
numberless as raindrops.

That's how I spent much of the day,
thinking of words to describe great splashes
of passing weeds. Bound for home
in the prodigal freshness of early May
when plum trees daub the slopes,
and every farmyard gives away a clump of lilacs,
their lavender just barely breaking
into the already overflowing morning,
I drove further and further away from a life
in which I'd had, I began to realize, only a small stake;
driving across Wisconsin and needing to speak
the right words about dandelions.

Blue-green oatstalks waved
in the wind off the North Sea
and sunshowers fell
like grace on his father's land.

That was before the bad trade:
after, his father recalled
the bartered farm each time
he went out in the mists.

Seagulls plucked what
they could from the turned
furrows. Was it he or they
that asked, How different?

A few things in the world
can exist without limit.
Like work: these fields could
never be cleared of stones.

Poverty—that was another.
So was a man's capacity
to choose wrong,
at least to make mistakes,

and so was the sea,
the frothing, ever-moving,
cold-enclosing ocean,
the island-wrapping sea.

This is what I burn: only windfall sticks,
silver maple being the usual.
Brittle and dry, it always lights quickly,
flames hot and high, then turns to powder ash.
Oak has earned a reputation for slow
and glowing heat. A length of it will last
probably ten times longer than maple
and its embers seem to breathe in the dark.
Yesterday, I found a small lilac branch,
freshly cut. I wondered if it could burn,
it was so thick with sap, whether or not
it would catch fire. But it did at once.
Nothing ethereal about the smoke:
summer nights when robins burble with song,
sumptuous mornings when leaves shine with light
and the memory of lavender blooms
at their most full. You stood close beside me
in the womanly trace of lilac smoke.

All Joyce Kilmer's clichés apply.
There are days when even a weed box elder
that was never planted, but rather, grew
from a spinner caught at the fence line,
can astonish. Forty feet tall, bent
and crooked, but nevertheless, a tree.
There are days when one can sit
and wonder at the thin blue of a late October
sky, and be made happy by the litter of leaves
across the cluttered yard, and by how
they curl as they dry, like curing tea.

Beauty inheres in curved things:
think of how, under
the bent surface of the sea,
whales in a dumb delicacy
move in a choreography of heartbreak.
They rise and fall to their own music,
graze one another's flanks,
nuzzling scarred hides.

Even these yams on my kitchen table
crimped in a dozen places
exude a primal rightness,
as if they belonged to some
underground jigsaw God alone
could have made or could solve.
They tune to a music
on the lowest of frequencies.

RUTABAGAS: A LOVE POEM

Rutabagas were new to me
when I first paired with Jean.
At Thanksgiving and Easter dinners
her grandpa Frank, her spinster cousin,
mom, dad, and a tribe of handsome
brothers dined in near silence
at a great green table
with fierce griffins underneath.
I would wonder if their quiet
was about secrets or something wrong
but now I think it was
just how they gathered.

Rutabagas were on the table.
I had to ask Jean what they were.
My first mouthful tasted
like something in a gunny sack;
nothing like a wine
from which an epicure, or would-be epicure,
might claim to read the soils
in which the grapes were grown.
She said she loved their dug-up texture,
the hint of dirt
that couldn't be baked away,
how they left the tongue
with a rumor of something
underground and dark.

Autumn vegetables suit her,
I think, and none more than rutabagas,
so reluctant to have left the ground.

FOR MY WIFE, DRIVING BACK FROM OHIO

I imagine you now,
still crossing Wisconsin
fifty or so miles east from here.
You are watching exit ramps vanish
in the rear-view mirror.

I do the waiting tasks,
dishes, and day-old newspapers.
At sunset I take out the trash.

Darkness tints the evening,
leeches into the sky
like paint off a brush rinsed
in a waterglass.
From near the backyard fence,

and surprising, so late in the fall,
a cricket starts its slow song
that is no song at all,

a record of seconds before dark.
I imagine you now, counting
mileposts the same way,
driving west on 94, each
a tired step nearer your end of day.

A ragged hour, shapeless as fear;
the wasting October light.
I need you here.

Getting the paper, unsure
if I am hungover or just sleep deprived,
I halt to study a blue jay, its blunt beak

picking among the still-sticky
seeds of pumpkin guts that lay
on the porch floor in a clump

of husks and strings, like medical waste.
A noisy, quarrelsome bird, yet
the pattern of its feathers, certain

as brush strokes on a china plate,
is decisive and tender at once.
I was as conscious of this bird's

presence as I would be of the rain
were I caught out in a storm; as conscious
as I am of color; of cold; of home.

A more focused man than me
could make a haiku out of a blue jay
on the porch, first thing in the morning.

There is a feeling you get when you are nearing home
after a long day driving back from South Dakota,
sort of like when, in a game of solitaire,
you realize, I know I'm going to win, and now
the needed nine or ace simply must turn up;
knowing that soon, one after another stilt of cards
will be shifted into place, and as if by nature,
the whole thing will play out as surely as a pink bud
in due course becomes a blossom and then an apple.
There is a feeling you get when you pass by this or that
street where you used to live, and know that now
it can never be anything except where you used to live.
There is a feeling, when, eight hours and 350 miles
after you started, you pull up at home and turn
the key back, and you sit there a minute
as the engine ticks and cools, and cools;
like you have just grown up all over again.

PLANTING NARCISSI
ON THE DAY OF THE DEAD

November first, and I am on my knees
immuring daffodils in the six-by-three
flower bed out front. What makes me happiest
this late afternoon is the sight of a bruise-colored
angleworm wriggling and waving half-out
of a wedge of dirt. Last night, we turned
the clocks back, a realignment
that saddens me, most years, but on
this welcome warm day the early dark
carries no dread. Night will fall as it should.
I am planting the bulbs I just
brought home, an impulse purchase
of an impulse flower, each brown nugget
a micro-Easter to be tucked away. The fact is,
I'll probably forget I planted these
until spring (just as I am sure the squirrel
I can see in the next yard will forget
the acorns it buries with equal earnestness).

On my knees not long before dark,
gratefully sprinkling bone meal.

The air was warm this afternoon
and stayed warm well into the evening;
and so we once again too soon
acted as if it were spring, leaving

windows open and putting the screen
in the door. A little after dark
the chill returns. The air that seemed
so soft a while ago now starts

to clutch at my ankles, cold
as the flat side of a wedge.
I rise to shut the door; of old
oak and glass with a beveled edge,

it has swung on the same hinges
since 1885.
I've shut it ten thousand times since
moving here with my child and wife

twenty years back. Across the street
stand homes that have been around
as long. I rarely meet
those folks yet, looking on

their houses and simply knowing
neighbors are also set about
their rounds of coming and going
from wherever they travel, I have no doubt

that this is my home, that I belong
here with my hand on the door.
The cliché runs, Time Marches On.
Just now, I think it stops—if only for

that moment before I turn
the deadbolt left and shut out
the cooling dark, before I return
to my spot on the couch.

Lifetimes are made of such daily stuff:
doors to be opened and shut, lights
we need to turn on and turn off;
welcome rhythms of day and night.

ACKNOWLEDGMENTS

I wish to thank the editors of the following publications, in which these poems originally appeared (sometimes in a slightly different form or under a different title):

Blueroad Reader I, "Outside Trotter's Café"
Clifden Anthology 32, "John McGahern's Childhood"
Cold Mountain Review, "Trapped Sparrow, O'Hare Airport"
Cortland Review, "Scenic Overlook"
The Cresset, "Waking up in the House of Men"
Emprise Review, "Blackbird in Beloit"
Great River Review, "Predictability" and "A Prayer in Midsummer"
Grey Sparrow, "Quiet" and "Troubling Myself with Things Too Great for Me"
If Bees Are Few: A Hive of Bee Poems (University of Minnesota Press, 2016), "Bumblebee in the Basement"
Natural Bridge, "The April Man" "Layers"
Nimrod, "Pain Management" and "Window Kills"
Poetry East, "Ordinary Sounds"
Potomac Review, "Edwin Muir's *An Autobiography*"
Salamander, "Late Night, in Kilkenny" and "Clotheslines"
Sundogs (Parallel Press, 2006), "For my Wife, Driving Back from Ohio"; "Rutabagas: A Love Poem"; " In Early Spring"; "Anemochory"; "The River Road, Again"; "Dandelions"; "On the Cannon River"; "Summer Evening"; "Butterfly in August"; and "Past Guessing"

JAMES SILAS ROGERS is the author of a chapbook, *Sundogs,* and of a collection of essays and poems involving cemeteries, *Northern Orchards: Places Near the Dead.* Four of his essays have been named "notables" in the *Best American Essays* volumes. His poems have appeared in many journals, including *Cortland Review, The Cresset, Poetry East, Nimrod, Natural Bridge,* and in several anthologies. He has also published widely on Irish-American literature and history.

The Collector of Shadows was designed and
set in type by Judy Gilats in Saint Paul, Minnesota.
The text face is Ten Oldstyle, drawn for the digital age
by Robert Slimbach, and the display face is
Proxima Nova, designed by Mark Simonson.

CPSIA information can be obtained
at www.ICGtesting.com
Printed in the USA
BVHW031324120322
631337BV00005B/110